21st Century Skills Library

LIFE SKILLS BIOGRAPHIES

BONO

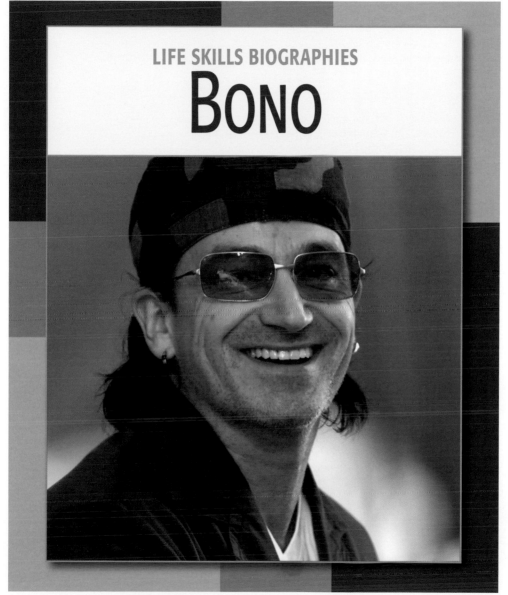

Christin Ditchfield

Cherry Lake Publishing
Ann Arbor, Michigan

Published in the United States of America by Cherry Lake Publishing
Ann Arbor, MI
www.cherrylakepublishing.com

Content Adviser: Dr. Chuck Berg, University of Kansas

Photo Credits: Cover and page 1, © Reuters/Corbis; page 6, © Soeren Stache/dpa/Corbis; pages 9, 16, and 19 © Corbis; pages 13, 21, 22, and 25, © Neal Preston/Corbis; page 15, © Virginia Turbett/Redferns/Retna Ltd.; page 27, © S.I.N./Corbis; page 29, © William Campbell/Sygma/Corbis; page 30, © Alessandro Bianchi/Reuters/Corbis; page 31, © Mike Hutchings/Reuters/Corbis; page 32 and 34, © Reuters/Corbis; page 36, Time & Life Pictures/Getty Images; page 37, Julien Behal/Pool/epa/Corbis; page 39, © Mario Anzuoni/Reuters/Corbis; page 40, © Brooks Kraft/Corbis; page 41, © Nancy Kaszerman/ZUMA/Corbis; page 42, © Mark Savage/Corbis

Library of Congress Cataloging-in-Publication Data
Ditchfield, Christin.
  Bono / Christin Ditchfield.
     p. cm. — (Life skills biographies)
  ISBN-13: 978-1-60279-066-7
  ISBN-10: 1-60279-066-3
  1. Bono, 1960– —Juvenile literature. 2. Rock musicians—Biography—Juvenile literature.
I. Title. II. Series.
  ML3930.B592D58 2008
  782.42166092—dc22
  [B]   2007012506

Cherry Lake Publishing would like to acknowledge the work of
The Partnership for 21st Century Skills.
Please visit www.21stcenturyskills.org for more information.

CONTENTS

INTRODUCTION

The name Paul Hewson means little to most people. But the name Bono is almost universally recognized. Paul Hewson started his life in Ireland and through determination, hard work—and more than a little talent— became Bono, the internationally known superstar and lead singer of the rock band U2. Over the years, U2 has been honored with more than 20 Grammy awards, an Oscar, and a Golden Globe. In 2005, the band was inducted into the Rock and Roll Hall of Fame.

Behind the sunglasses, the rock and roll image, and the fame, however, lies a husband and father who has struggled to find his way through great personal tragedy, difficult family relationships, and more. Not content to rest on his achievements as a member of U2, he has used his fame and influence to reach celebrities, politicians, and everyday people all over the world. His passion for the cause of helping the poverty- and AIDS-stricken people of Africa has motivated millions to develop and contribute to finding solutions to the problems that plague the African continent. His commitment and leadership have resulted in his being granted honorary knighthood. He has also been nominated for the Nobel Peace Prize three times.

Bono's determination to overcome personal adversity and change the world for the better has been an inspiration to people everywhere.

CHAPTER ONE

SOMETHING MISSING

*Paul Hewson, better known as Bono, was
born in Dublin, Ireland, in 1960.*

"*You don't become a rock star unless you've got something missing
somewhere. . . . If you were of sound mind or a more complete person, you
could feel normal without 70,000 people a night screaming their love for
you.*"—Bono

Millions of people know him as Bono—the lead singer of the world-
famous rock band U2. His parents named him Paul David Hewson. He was
born in Dublin, Ireland, on May 10, 1960. Paul discovered the joy of making

music at an early age. When he was a toddler, he loved to stand under his grandmother's piano to listen to its sounds reverberate. "I remember putting my hand up and pressing the keyboard and hearing a note, and then pressing another note, playing with it the way kids do, just making noise," he says. "I could almost, even then, hear the melodies in the air."

Paul's friends and family remember him as a noisy, mischievous, freckle-faced kid—full of excitement and energy. A natural leader, he made friends easily and was popular in school. He played chess like a champion and even competed at the international level. He enjoyed playing football (which Americans call soccer) just as much.

Growing up, Paul was surrounded by beautiful sounds. He heard Irish folk music and hymn singing at his grandmother's house. His aunts, uncles, and cousins made sure there was music at every family party or celebration. Paul's father, Bob, loved opera. After work or on the weekends, Bob would stand in front of the stereo speakers, singing along with his favorite songs and "conducting" an imaginary orchestra with his wife's knitting needles. Yet surprisingly, it never occurred to him to encourage either of his two sons to pursue music.

Paul's older brother, Norman, had a guitar. Norman taught himself to play some of the rock and roll sounds of Jimi Hendrix, The Beatles, and The Who. Paul wanted to learn how to play the guitar, too. He begged his parents to let him take music lessons, but they didn't see any point to it. So he did his best to pick out a few chords on his own.

When Paul's grandmother decided to sell her piano, Paul pleaded with his mother, Iris, to keep the piano at their house. Iris didn't understand

The boy who grew up to become Bono still doesn't understand why his father didn't share his love of music with him. If music meant so much to Bob, why didn't he see what it meant to his son? "It's so odd, it's the thing I can't figure out," Bono said. "It was almost like my father's whole attitude was: Don't dream. That was his unspoken and sometimes spoken advice. To dream is to be disappointed. . . . He had given up his dreams, so he didn't want me to fill my head with mine."

Paul, however, decided he would devote his life to dreaming big dreams and finding ways to make those dreams come true. He would never, ever give them up.

Today, whether he is creating cutting-edge sounds for U2 or organizing international efforts to end world hunger, Bono is all about big ideas. He has lived an extraordinary life because he has dared to dream.

why he felt so strongly about it. "We don't have any room!" she said. And that was that.

At a parent-teacher conference, the principal of Paul's elementary school suggested Paul join the school choir. Unfortunately, Paul didn't get a chance to say "Yes!" His mother answered for him: "No thanks! That's not something Paul would be interested in." She had no idea how badly he wanted to sing. For some reason, Paul didn't speak up.

He didn't know how to tell his parents what he was feeling or how to make them understand. And somehow they didn't realize that music was his greatest passion. It would take a few years for Paul to find his voice—to learn how to express the music he heard inside of him.

In spite of some disappointment and discouragement, Paul's childhood was not unhappy. His parents were good, decent, hardworking people. The house was full of Bob's music and Iris's laughter, and the love the family shared.

But when Paul was 14, his world came crashing down. The entire family had gathered to celebrate his grandparents' 50th wedding anniversary. That night, after the party, his grandfather suddenly had a heart attack and died. A few days later, at the funeral, Paul's mother collapsed. She had to be rushed to the hospital. Doctors determined that Iris had suffered a brain **hemorrhage**. There was nothing they could do for her. A few days later, she died.

The Hewson family was in shock. Full of his own heartache and pain, Paul's father didn't know how to help his sons. He

When Bono was a young boy, he didn't know how to make his parents understand how passionate he was about music.

didn't know what to say to them, so he didn't say anything at all. After her funeral, he never talked about Iris again.

"My mother died and then there were just three men living on their own in a house. That is all it was then, it ceased being a home," Paul later

Norman was eight years older than Paul. Norman had always looked out for his little brother, trying to help and encourage him and set a good example for him. But after Iris's death, the brothers found themselves fighting constantly. Sometimes the fights got physical.

Paul later said about Norman: "I remember once we had a big fight, and I threw a knife at him. I didn't throw it to kill him; I just threw it to scare him. And it stuck into the door. . . . And I realized that I didn't mean to but I could have killed him." Both brothers burst into tears. In that moment, they admitted that they had a serious problem. They weren't communicating their thoughts and feelings to each other. They made the choice to speak clearly and effectively and to stop taking their anger out on each other. They decided to share responsibility for how they expressed themselves.

said. "It was just a house with three men killing each other slowly, not knowing what to do with our sense of loss and just taking it out on each other."

They were trying to escape the memories, each in his own way. The Hewson men hated coming home to the emptiness, the hurt, and the pain. "Our mother was gone, the beautiful Iris," Paul said. "I felt abandoned and afraid. I guess fear converts to anger pretty quickly. It's still with me."

Paul started skipping school and getting into trouble. His anger often raged out of control. He also was experiencing memory loss. As he would think back over a previous week, he couldn't recall if he'd actually *done* a particular thing or just dreamed about it. It frightened him.

Finally, Paul went to the school guidance counselor for help. He sat in the counselor's office and talked nonstop for almost an entire day. He poured out all the thoughts and feelings he'd kept inside since his mother's death. The counselor listened with care and concern. After a while, the counselor recommended that Paul talk to a **psychologist**. It helped Paul to talk about his feelings, to share with someone else what he was going through.

Still, Paul was a troubled teenager with a lot of questions about life and death and faith. He says he often went back and forth between hope and despair. He couldn't find anything to fill the emptiness he felt inside. There were moments when his pain and suffering—and the suffering he saw in the world around him—made him think of committing suicide. Paul remembers a lovely woman at church saying to him, "Yes, we live in a fallen world, but it's still beautiful. God's fingerprints are everywhere if you want to see them."

Like Paul, many students with problems turn to their guidance counselors for help.

Those words had a great impact on him. "In despair, I did pray to God. And I discovered that even sometimes in the silence, God does answer. The answer may not be the one you want to hear, but there's always an answer, if you are serious, if you are ready to let go," Paul said. "I got to a place in my life where I wanted to make some sort of spiritual sense of the world. I put out those prayers because I really did think that my head was going to explode. . . . And then two things happened in the same few weeks and they both saved my life."

Paul Hewson would never be the same.

Many people turn to prayer during times of crisis. Paul Hewson turned to prayer in an attempt to make some sense of his life.

CHAPTER TWO

A VISION OF THE FUTURE

Bono (right) met his wife, Alison (middle), in 1976

"There was a heat haze coming off the back of Reggie's bike, and she looked like she was in a pool of water, walking through it. There was something so still about her, and to a person who is not still, it was the most attractive thing in the world." —Bono, upon seeing his future wife for the first time

In 1976, two years after his mother's death, 16-year-old Paul was still struggling to find his way. Then suddenly he had what he called "a vision of my future." Paul and his friend Reggie were skipping school. As Paul climbed onto the back of Reggie's motorcycle, a beautiful girl caught his eye.

"I thought she looked Spanish, a rose for sure, dark with blood red lips . . . this quiet mysterious girl who was so unself-conscious, she was completely unaware that she was attractive." As restless as he was, Paul couldn't help being drawn to the peace he felt in the presence of this girl named Alison. Within a few weeks, Paul and Ali were dating. Within a few years, they would be married. "I always felt more myself with her than anybody," Paul said. "When you've got that sort of thing you should never let it go."

Meanwhile, Paul was still just getting to know Ali when he met the three other people who would change his life forever. Larry Mullen Jr. was a new student at Mount Temple High School, Paul's school. Larry played the drums—and he wanted to start a band. He put up a notice on the school bulletin board. Larry found out that his fellow students, David "the Edge" Evans and Adam Clayton, both played the guitar, and someone told Larry to talk to Paul Hewson. Paul could often be seen playing the guitar around the school campus—usually surrounded by a group of pretty girls. The four guys met for the first time after school at Larry's house.

Paul showed up without a guitar—he didn't actually have one of his own. It turned out that he could barely play at all. But what Paul lacked in skill, he made up for in passion and intensity. When he walked into a room, he automatically took charge. Larry remembers that Paul's leadership of the band began during that first rehearsal: "It was the Larry Mullen Band for about ten minutes so as not to hurt my feelings. It was also my kitchen. Then Bono came in and that was the end of that."

Paul became the lead singer almost by default. Nobody else wanted the job. Edge and Adam were clearly better guitar players. "I had a few chords, a few songs I could play," Paul remembers. "The idea of wanting to sing, I don't

Paul met Larry Mullen Jr. when Larry was trying to start a band.

remember when that happened. I mean I had always wanted to sing, but I don't remember owning up to it."

The guys decided to get together every week to practice their music. They wanted to be able to play a few songs at the school talent show later in the year. The more time they spent together, the more they found they had in common. They soon became close friends.

Paul and his bandmates liked to give each other crazy nicknames.

The guys enjoyed giving each other crazy nicknames, just for fun. One of Paul's first nicknames was "Steinhegvanhuysenolegbangbangbang." It was shortened to "Houseman." Eventually, it became "Bono Vox," a name they saw on a sign advertising Bonavox, a brand of hearing aids. The guys teased Paul that the name was perfect for him, because he always sang so loudly—as though he thought his audience needed hearing aids. Later,

Bono realized it really was a good fit. The words came from a Latin phrase meaning "good voice."

Whenever they met to rehearse, band members brought with them the latest music they had discovered—songs and artists with sounds they liked. They were trying to find a style that fit them. They started out playing covers—their own versions of popular songs written and performed by other rock groups. But as the members of the band say now, they weren't really good enough musicians to be able to play the songs properly. So they decided to start writing their own music.

Once again, Bono took the lead. Although later he was quick to point out that each member of the band contributed to the end result, Bono was the one who usually came up with the melodies to begin with. He wrote the lyrics to nearly all of the band's songs.

As the day of the talent show drew near, the band realized they needed

Learning & Innovation Skills

Songwriting opened up a whole new world to Bono. "I started to use music as a way of really expressing what was going on in my head," he recalls. In his music, he could pour out all his anger and rebellion and frustration and fear. Many of Bono's first songs were about his mother's death. In others, he shared how difficult he found it to talk with his father. In his songs, he described his love for Ali, his faith in God, and his struggles to become the kind of man he wanted to be. Bono also wrote songs about important social and political issues.

"It is such an extraordinary thing, music," he says. "It seems to be how we communicate on another level. If you believe that we contain within our skin and bones a spirit that might last longer than your time breathing in and out, music is the thing that wakes it up. It certainly woke mine up. I wasn't looking for grace, but luckily grace was looking for me."

Bono's originality and inventiveness are expressed through his music. What are some other creative ways to express your thoughts and feelings?

a name. At first, they chose Feedback. Later they would call themselves The Hype. Although they say they played very badly, the guys remember how the girls in the school gymnasium went wild. From the moment the band heard the screaming and cheering, they were hooked. There was something incredibly powerful about the experience of performing live onstage, connecting with people through music. Bono says, "Everything changed for me, because now I knew what I wanted to do for the rest of my life. There it was, the thing I didn't know. And that happened so quickly. Suddenly you have a reason to be."

Over the next four years, the band members worked hard to become better musicians and to learn the ins and outs of the music industry. They started developing their own unique sound, rather than simply imitating the sounds of other bands. They began performing at high school and college dances, county fairs and music festivals, talent contests and community concerts. At bigger events, they were often invited to play a few songs to warm up the audience for more accomplished and successful bands.

After a while, the guys started sounding better than some of the bands they were opening for, but they still had a long way to go. Their future manager, Paul McGuinness, remembers: "They were doing then badly, what they now do well. Bono was very unusual in that he was at the front of the stage, trying to engage the audience, to get them to look in his eyes. Most other singers at that time were looking anywhere but at the audience."

In 1978, the band decided it was time for a new name. A friend put together a list of six or seven names for them to choose from. The one they settled on was U2. It wasn't Bono's favorite, and when he realized

The members of U2 are, from left, guitarist The Edge (David Evans), bass player Adam Clayton, lead singer Bono, and drummer Larry Mullen Jr.

it was a kind of pun ("You, too!"), he liked it even less. Still, it was kind of cool and mysterious-sounding, as though it could mean all kinds of things—and more important, it could easily fit in large type on tickets, programs, and signs.

People in the music industry started paying attention to U2. The band came into contact with reporters, agents, managers, and music producers who saw its **potential**. They offered the members of the band encouragement and advice. With the prize money from a local contest,

Bono, Larry, Edge, and Adam were only teenagers when they first formed the band. They were young and wild and liked to party. As more and more opportunities opened up for them, things got pretty exciting. Suddenly, the band had an inside look at the rock and roll lifestyle, with all its privileges and temptations.

Early on, U2's members decided there were some things they would do differently from other bands. Every time they stepped onstage, they wanted to give their best performance. By the time they hit it big, most of the members of the band were married, with young children. They did not want drugs to be a part of the behind-the-scenes atmosphere on their tours. And they would not allow anyone associated with the band to take advantage of the young people—especially girls—who hung around backstage.

In a world of "sex, drugs, and rock and roll," U2 was determined to show respect for their music, for their fans, and for their families.

U2 had its first publicity photos taken. Band members bought new "rock star" outfits for performing onstage. And they recorded a demo—a sample of their music to send to concert promoters, radio stations, and record producers.

In 1980, U2 released its first full album, *Boy*. That was followed by *October*, then *War*, and *Under a Blood Red Sky*. Though still an up-and-coming young band, they were performing at events all over Great Britain and Europe—and even in the United States. Ali often traveled with the band. She and Bono were married in 1982.

In 1984, U2 released its fifth album, *The Unforgettable Fire*. That same year, the band was invited to headline the Amnesty International "Conspiracy of Hope" tour. The following year, Bono was asked to join some of rock music's legends and superstars to record a song for charity: the Band Aid single, "Do They Know It's Christmas Time/Feed the World." Then U2 performed in

U2 performs at the Live Aid benefit concert in 1985.

the Live Aid mega benefit concert broadcast on television and radio into millions of homes all over the world. In the middle of one of their songs, Bono suddenly jumped off the stage, over the security barriers, and into the audience to dance with a fan. It was a moment that everyone watching would remember as one of the highlights of the event.

Still in his early twenties, Bono had achieved success beyond anything he could have imagined when he first joined Larry, Edge, and Adam for a band rehearsal in Larry's kitchen. And this was just the beginning.

CHAPTER THREE

U2—"ROCK'S HOTTEST TICKET"

This portrait of U2 was taken in 1987 during the Joshua Tree Tour.

"There's nothing like being number one, there really isn't. . . . There's no feeling quite like it in the world. Everything terrible that ever happened to you in your life is no longer terrible in that moment."—Bono

In 1987, U2 released a new album, *The Joshua Tree*. With songs such as "Running to Stand Still," "With or Without You," and "I Still Haven't Found What I'm Looking For," the album raced up the *Billboard* charts to number one. Suddenly, Bono, Larry, Adam, and Edge were international rock superstars.

Music critics described *The Joshua Tree* as *the* classic rock album of the 1980s—"an awe-inspiring landmark." It combined a raw, "hungry" rock sound with deeply soulful, spiritual lyrics. *The Joshua Tree* would go on to sell more than 20 million copies, and land at number 26 on *Rolling Stone* magazine's list of the top 500 albums of all time.

U2 earned a reputation for putting on incredible live shows. Bono had explosive energy onstage. No one—not even the other members of the band—knew what he would do. Bono later explained, "For U2, every night has to be the best night. And if it isn't, there has to be a reason. We have very high standards and we always remember who pays our wages. Our audience deserves the best. . . . I can feel if the crowd is losing interest and I might just throw a firecracker into that part of the crowd, and the firecracker would probably be me. Light the fuse, see what happens."

For two years, the band toured all across the United States, Great Britain, Europe, and Asia. They played to packed houses every night, selling out arenas and stadiums. *Time* featured U2 on the cover of its magazine, with the headline: "Rock's Hottest Ticket."

U2 wasn't content to rest on the success of *The Joshua Tree*. With their next few albums, the band members were really pushing themselves to keep learning and growing as musicians. They experimented with new sounds

On Bono's birthday—May 10—in 1989, he received a very special present. Ali gave birth to the couple's first child, a little girl they named Jordan. "What a great gift she has turned out to be," Bono says. "We are very close, Jordan and I."

Bono's second daughter, Memphis Eve, was born in 1993. His son, Elijah, came along in 1999. John was born in 2001.

In the midst of all the craziness of the rock and roll celebrity life, Bono says his family keeps him grounded. He knows that being a parent requires leadership, responsibility, and accountability. He also recognizes that having a family requires him to be flexible and adaptable so he can meet his children's needs.

and styles of music. Their next album, *Rattle and Hum*, wasn't as well received as they had hoped. But in 1991, the band members reinvented themselves with a "darker, funkier, sexier" sound on the album *Achtung Baby*. It earned U2 a Grammy award for Best Rock Performance. And in 1993, the band tried something completely different on *Zooropa*—which won Grammy awards for Best Alternative Rock Album and Best Music Video, Long Form.

For the "*Zooropa*/Zoo TV" concert tour, the band developed a huge production with elaborate sets and mind-blowing special effects. Bono threw himself wholeheartedly into the process. He created a series of outlandish characters that he would pretend to be onstage—complete with crazy costumes and heavy makeup. He appeared as a stereotypical rock star called The Fly; a corrupt **televangelist** known as The Mirrorball Man; and the devil as an aging rock god—Mister Mephisto. Adam, Edge, and Larry dressed up in costumes, too. Some fans didn't know quite what to make of this new U2. But Bono was loving every minute of it. "It was a thrilling, very creative time," he says. "We were lost to our work and our art, and life all seemed to blur into one."

Bono performs as The Fly, one of the characters he created for the Zooropa/Zoo TV tour.

Bono was invited to sing duets with such music legends as Frank Sinatra, Johnny Cash, Roy Orbison, B. B. King, and Luciano Pavarotti. In fact, many of the musicians Bono admired when he was a child were now his friends. Rock stars who pioneered the kind of music that inspired U2 were now asking Bono to write songs for them or to perform on their albums. It was amazing to discover that U2's fans included all kinds of famous and important people—supermodels and celebrity athletes, movie stars and politicians. They invited U2 to their parties, premieres, and special events, hoping to spend a little time with the members of their favorite band.

Although they had achieved unbelievable success—with more to come—it wasn't all wonderful. The band had its share of problems, personally and professionally. They were the first to admit that they had made plenty of mistakes. Not every musical experiment turned out well. The *Zooropa*/Zoo TV tour was so expensive to produce that it almost sent the band into bankruptcy. Some of their albums didn't quite live up to their hopes. Either they weren't able to get the sound they were trying to achieve, or the message of the songs fell flat. Critics said the band was too full of itself, too preachy, too religious, and too political. Fans who appreciated hearing Bono speak openly about his Christian faith were confused by the characters he played in concert. When he wrote songs from the perspective of people who didn't share his values or beliefs, they thought he was abandoning his own faith.

Bono realizes now that he made a huge mistake when he decided to start smoking in his thirties. At the time, he liked the gravelly edge it gave his voice. Then he started losing his voice in concerts and recording sessions. There were times he wasn't able to sing at all. He knew if he didn't stop, it could end his career.

And there were other temptations that threatened to destroy what was precious to him. "It's not easy to deal with money," Bono says. "It's not easy

Bono has performed with many other musicians. Here
he performs with tenor Luciano Pavarotti in 1995.

to deal with fame, it's not easy to deal with women throwing themselves at you, even being married, perhaps especially being married. No matter how strong you are, no matter how upright, these are real hurdles that you have to figure out how to get over."

Learning & Innovation Skills

As a lead singer and songwriter—and someone with a truly larger-than-life personality—Bono often gets the most media attention, the most fan mail, the most credit for the success of U2. But he insists that it is not a one-man show. All of U2's efforts have been a collaboration.

"I need this band. The truth is I need them more than they need me. I'm a lousy guitar player and an even lousier piano player. Had I not got Edge close by who was an extraordinarily gifted complex musician, I would be hopeless. Had I not got Larry and Adam, the melodies would not be grounded. . . . They raise my game."

He adds, "Four brains are better than one. It's a lot less lonely and often much more fun. And . . . it's a rare privilege to be in the company of people who you started out with. . . . We bring the best out of each other not the worst, which is what a lot of bands do."

It is almost unheard of in the rock and roll world, but 30 years after their first rehearsal, Bono, Larry, Adam, and Edge are still in the band. And they're still best friends.

After years of nonstop touring, the band was burned out—empty and exhausted. They decided to take a break. They needed to rest and relax and spend time with their families. Since he was a teenager, Bono had been on the road. He had to ask a friend for advice on how to live a "normal" life that included getting into a daily routine at home. Things like having a cup of coffee and reading the newspaper in the morning, taking the kids to school, going to church on Sundays, and having friends over for dinner afterward were all new to him. He loved his time off! But he couldn't slow down for long.

CHAPTER FOUR

"THE GIRL WITH THE BEARD"

We slept in a tent. In the morning, as the mist would lift, we would see thousands of people walking in lines toward the camp, people who had been walking for great distances through the night—men, women, children, families who'd lost everything, taking a few possessions on a voyage to meet mercy."—Bono, recalling his trip to an Ethiopian refugee camp

Refugee camps in Ethiopia and elsewhere are crowded and dirty. Bono's trip to visit a refugee camp changed his life.

Bono and his wife, Ali, lived in a refugee camp for three weeks and gained a new understanding of the horror of poverty and disease.

The year before *The Joshua Tree* made U2 international superstars, Bono received an invitation from the president of World Vision to join a relief work campaign in Ethiopia. Bono and his wife, Ali, spent three weeks living in a tent in a refugee camp, handing out food and clothing and medical supplies. They wrote little songs and stories and plays to teach the Ethiopian families about proper health care and hygiene. No one at the camp knew that Bono was an up-and-coming Irish rock singer. The children saw his long hair and earrings and unshaven face and called him "The Girl With The Beard."

For Bono and Ali, it was a life-changing experience. Bono had always wanted to reach out to needy people in war-torn and poverty-stricken countries. From the beginning, U2 had regularly performed charity concerts and fund-raising events. Many of their songs spoke of the horrors of poverty, starvation, and disease. They condemned injustice, prejudice, and war. The band had experienced some of these things firsthand growing up in Ireland, a country torn apart by conflict between Catholics and Protestants. There were bombings and drive-by shootings and other acts of terror in their own neighborhoods. Bono himself was the product of a "mixed" marriage—his father was Catholic and his mother was Protestant. The Hewsons knew all about being caught in the middle of a dangerous world.

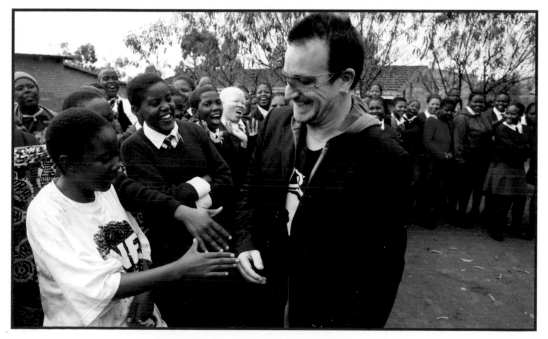

Bono visits a school in Lesotho. He continues to reach out to people living with poverty and disease, especially in Africa.

But the trip to Ethiopia opened Bono's eyes like never before. For the first time, he saw just how brutal the suffering of the African people was. He couldn't get the images out of his head. As time went on, Bono became less content to sing a few songs about the suffering or to help raise a little money now and then. He had to do more.

Bono realized that his fame and fortune gave him great influence. Not only could he urge U2's fans to vote and give money and get involved. He also had access to the many celebrities and politicians and powerful people he had met over the years. He could approach world leaders, and because

Bono dances with an orphan in Uganda who is living with HIV/AIDS.

of his reputation and the media attention that followed him everywhere, these leaders would listen to him.

Bono could see that the people of **third world**, or developing, countries in Africa face many challenges. They have little access to nutritious food, clothing, shelter, health care, and education. Their governments are often corrupt, **repressive**, or deeply in debt to other countries. They are dependent on welfare programs and foreign aid. Third world countries have not developed the kinds of businesses, industries, and trade relationships that would enable them to support themselves and their people.

But there is an even bigger problem: more than 19 million Africans have died of **AIDS**, and another 24 million are living with the disease. Thirteen million children have lost both parents to AIDS. Many African people have not been taught how to prevent the disease. They have many misconceptions about how it spreads. Too often, those who are diagnosed with AIDS cannot afford medication or treatment. Or adequate treatment just isn't available.

21st Century Content

In 2002, Bono helped create an organization called DATA. It stands for Debt, AIDS, Trade, Africa.

DATA raises awareness of the problems the people of Africa face by organizing trips to Africa for high-profile celebrities such as Bob Geldof and Chris Tucker, as well as noted politicians and journalists. DATA has also brought African activists to the United States to tour with celebrities such as Ashley Judd, Warren Buffet, and Lance Armstrong. Media coverage of these trips draws attention to the crises Africans face. DATA believes that the more people are made aware of the problems, the more they will get involved in finding solutions—and the more they will pressure their national governments to do the same.

For the past 10 years, Bono has worked tirelessly to draw attention to the needs of the African people, to raise awareness and money to help the poorest of the poor. In 1999, Bono met with U.S. president Bill Clinton, British prime minister Tony Blair, and Pope John Paul II as part of the Jubilee 2000 campaign for third world debt relief. He spoke before the United Nations and U.S. Congress, urging world leaders to forgive the debts of poverty-stricken countries that would never be able to repay them anyway.

Bono met with Pope John Paul II (seated) and other world leaders as part of a campaign for third world debt relief.

Then in 2002, Bono joined President George W. Bush at the White House to announce a new $5 billion aid package designed to help the world's poorest countries that respect human rights. "This is an important first step," Bono said, "and a serious and impressive new level of commitment. . . . This must happen urgently, because this is a crisis."

Though he continued to be outspoken in his views on other controversial issues, Bono insisted that having compassion for the poor and needy wasn't about politics. He refused to take sides or criticize any political party that was willing to step up to the plate. And when he spoke at the National Prayer Breakfast in Washington, D.C., Bono reminded everyone that people of all faiths are called to reach out to those who are suffering.

To a new generation, Bono had become more well known as an **activist** than as a musician. Teenagers who didn't know any U2 songs knew all about Bono and AIDS and Africa. Once again, the Irish rock star was featured on the cover of *Time* magazine. This time, the headline asked, "Can Bono Save the World?"

CHAPTER FIVE

SURPRISED BY JOY

Time *magazine featured Bono on its cover in March 2002.*

"To be surprised by joy is the most wonderful thing, to be reminded that your heart is pumping blood around your body and your eyes are awake to what's going on in the world and what's happening to you, and to give thanks. . . ." —Bono

In January 2007, in a special ceremony in Dublin, Ireland, Bono became an honorary Knight Commander of the Order of the British Empire. He was awarded the honorary title in recognition of his contributions to the world of music and his humanitarian efforts in Africa.

With U2, he had already won more than 20 Grammy awards, an Oscar, and a Golden Globe. The band had been inducted into the Rock and Roll Hall of Fame. U2's most recent albums, *All That You Can't Leave Behind* and *How to Dismantle an Atomic Bomb* were tremendous successes. One of the singles, "Vertigo," was a smash hit worldwide. And the "Vertigo" concert tour drew more than 3 million people to 90 sold-out concerts.

Bono holds his honorary knighthood award. The title was awarded to recognize his musical contributions and humanitarian work in Africa.

In spite of all the praise and recognition, Bono says he is a deeply flawed man who still has much to learn.

"One of the extraordinary [things] that happens in your spiritual life is not that your character flaws go away, but they start to work for you," he says. "[If you've got] a big mouth: you end up a singer. You're insecure: you end up a performer who needs applause. I have heard of people having life-changing, miraculous turn-arounds, people set free from addiction after a single prayer. . . . But [for me] it . . . is probably more accurate to say, 'I was really lost, I'm a little less so at the moment.' And then a little less and a little less again. That to me is the spiritual life. It has slowly rebuilt me in a better image. It has taken years though, and it is not over yet."

In addition to knighthood, Bono has received the **prestigious** NAACP (National Association for the Advancement of Colored People) Image Award. Along with world leaders, presidents, and politicians, the rock star has been nominated for a **Nobel Peace Prize** three times. Today, Bono is arguably one of the most famous and influential people on the planet.

It's not surprising to U2 bandmate Larry Mullen. "Bono has always been larger than life," Larry says. "He brings a lot to those who know him. He's very generous and rather good company. He is also extremely complex. You don't know what is going on in that head of his and you might not want to. He has an explosive, unpredictable side to him. He's got an insatiable appetite for adventure and he will do almost anything and go anywhere to satisfy that."

Larry adds, "Being as successful as he is has real downsides, the opportunities afforded him are mind-blowing, the responsibility that comes with it is immense. It is extraordinary how he can survive and thrive on it. His faith is his anchor and I think that's what enables him to navigate his way through and come out relatively

Bono accepts the NAACP Image award from Tyra Banks in 2007.

unscathed. Unfortunately, the more successful and famous he becomes outside U2, the harder it is to get an opportunity to talk and hang out the way we used to, but that's life."

Bono's political and social activism leave him with less time for his music and bandmates. That is something he is working to change.

Bono understands that his passion for worldwide social and political causes has kept him from giving the band his full attention in recent years. At times, it has been difficult for Larry, Adam, and Edge. And that's something Bono wants to change—for his own sake, as well as that of his friends.

"Sometimes it comes across as if I got into U2 to save the world. I got into U2 to save myself," he says. "My gift is that I'm a singer, a songwriter and a performer. I just happened to have learned other skills to protect

U2 was inducted into the Rock and Roll Hall of Fame in 2005.

Bono has touched many lives with his music and with his commitment to making a difference in the world.

that gift, and those skills seem to suit political activism. But I am most excited about getting lost in the music again. In the near future, I am going to close the door on activism and commerce and other ideas that engage me, and I am going to shut it quite tight, for a little while at least, and focus on writing and making music."

That will mean spending a lot more time with the other members of U2. "I need the band," Bono says. "I am a better person for having been around these men. . . . I'm sure I've given them all headaches, heartaches, and anxiety attacks—and a lot of sleepless nights. But I also like to think I've given them a few laughs and some adventure."

As much as he says he plans to step back from campaigning for social causes, it hasn't happened yet. Bono keeps finding ideas, projects, and efforts that need his support. It appears that his legacy—his greatest contribution to the world—will not be the songs he has sung or the albums he has sold. It will be the countless hearts and lives that have been changed by his compassion and his commitment to speak out and make a difference in the world.

21st Century Content

Former North Carolina senator Jesse Helms told *Time* magazine, "When I was first told in 2000 that Bono wanted to meet with me to talk about boosting U.S. aid to Africa, I didn't know who he was. But my Senate staff certainly did. After so many years in Washington, I had met enough people to quickly figure out who is genuine and who is there for show. I knew as soon as I met Bono that he was genuine. He had his facts in hand and [wanted to do] all he could to help people in desperate need. . . . Bono helped me understand the scope of the tragedy in Africa, especially the pain it is bringing to infants and children and their families."

As a result, Senator Helms decided to get involved. He joined with Tennessee senator Bill Frist to create and help pass a bill that would provide $200 million to fight AIDS in Africa.

TIMELINE

1960   Bono is born Paul David Hewson on May 10, in Dublin, Ireland.

1974   Paul's mother, Iris, dies suddenly of a brain hemorrhage.

1976   Paul joins Larry Mullen Jr., David Evans, and Adam Clayton to form the band that will become U2.

1980   U2 releases its first album, *Boy*.

1981   U2 releases its second album, *October*.

1982   Bono marries his teenage sweetheart, Alison Stewart.

1983   U2 releases its third album, *War*, and its fourth, *Under a Blood Red Sky*.

1984   The band records a fifth album, *The Unforgettable Fire*, and headlines the Amnesty International "Conspiracy of Hope" tour.

1985   Bono joins rock superstars to record the Band Aid single, "Do They Know It's Christmas Time/Feed the World;" U2 performs in the Live Aid mega benefit concert.

1986   Bono and Ali spend three weeks volunteering as relief workers with World Vision in Ethiopia.

1987   U2's album *The Joshua Tree* races to the top of the *Billboard* charts and earns two Grammy awards. The band appears on the cover of *Time* magazine.

1988   The band receives two more Grammy awards for Best Rock Performance by a Duo or Group and Best Performance Music Video.

1989   Bono becomes a father when his first child, daughter Jordan, is born on his birthday.

1991   U2 reinvents itself with the release of the critically acclaimed album, *Achtung Baby*.

1992   The band receives a Grammy award for Best Rock Performance, for *Achtung Baby*.

1993 Bono's second daughter, Eve, is born; U2 wins a Grammy award for Best Alternative Rock Album for the experimental sounds of *Zooropa*.

1994 "Zoo TV" earns U2 a Grammy award for Best Music Video, Long Form.

1995 Bono writes "Miss Sarajevo," to be sung by opera great Luciano Pavarotti.

1999 Bono meets with U.S. president Bill Clinton, British prime minister Tony Blair, and Pope John Paul II as part of the Jubilee 2000 campaign for third world debt relief; Bono's third child and first son, Elijah, is born.

2000 U2 releases the album *All That You Can't Leave Behind* and earns three more Grammy awards.

2001 Bono's fourth child, John, is born; U2 wins four more Grammy awards; Bono's father, Bob Hewson, dies of cancer.

2002 U2 performs during halftime at the Super Bowl; the cover of *Time* magazine asks, "Can Bono Save the World?"

2003 Bono is nominated for the Nobel Peace Prize for his work on third world debt relief and AIDS awareness.

2004 U2 releases the album *How to Dismantle an Atomic Bomb;* in the first deal of its kind, the band collaborates with Apple to create a U2 i-Pod and use the MP3 player to debut the single "Vertigo."

2005 U2 is inducted into the Rock and Roll Hall of Fame; Bono and Bill and Melinda Gates are named *Time* magazine's Persons of the Year; Bono is again nominated for the Nobel Peace Prize.

2006 Bono is nominated for the Nobel Peace Prize for the third time.

2007 Bono becomes an honorary Knight Commander of the Order of the British Empire.

Glossary

activist (AK-tuh-vist) a person who urges that strong action be taken to help or support a particular cause

AIDS (aydz) Acquired Immunodeficiency Syndrome; an illness in which the body's ability to protect itself against disease is destroyed

collaboration (kuh-lab-uh-RAY-shuhn) working together to do something

hemorrhage (HEM-ur-ij) severe, uncontrolled bleeding from a damaged blood vessel

humanitarian (hyoo-MAN-uh-TARE-ee-uhn) someone who helps suffering people

Nobel Peace Prize (noh-BEL PEESS PRIZE) annual prize created by Alfred Nobel; it is awarded to those whose achievements have advanced peace in the world

potential (puh-TEN-shuhl) what someone is capable of achieving in the future

prestigious (pre-STEE-juhs) highly respected; known for being important, powerful, or successful

psychologist (sye-KOL-uh-jist) a doctor who is trained to treat emotional and mental illness

repressive (ri-PRE-siv) something that severely limits freedom

reverberate (ree-VUR-buh-rate) to echo loudly and repeatedly

televangelist (tel-uh-VAN-juh-list) a preacher who conducts regularly televised religious programs

third world (THURD WURLD) the poor, underdeveloped countries of the world

For More Information

Books

Bono. *On The Move*. Nashville, TN: W Publishing Group, 2007.

Ellis, Deborah. *Our Stories, Our Songs: African Children Talk about AIDS*. Markham, ON, Canada: Fitzhenry and Whiteside, Limited, Publishers, 2005.

Hogan, Edward Patrick. *Ireland*. New York: Chelsea House, 2003.

Schaffer, David. *People in the News: Bono*. New York: Thomson Gale, 2003.

Web Sites

The Official Website of U2
www.u2.com
Offers news and information about the band, its history, photos and memorabilia, album covers, song lyrics, and a schedule of upcoming concerts and events.

DATA (Debt, AIDS, Trade, Africa)
www.data.org
Site of the organization founded by Bono in 2002 to raise awareness about the crises facing the people of Africa.

INDEX

ABOUT THE AUTHOR

Christin Ditchfield is the host of the internationally syndicated radio program *Take It To Heart!*® She is an accomplished educator, a popular conference speaker, and the author of more than 50 books. Christin writes on a wide variety of topics, ranging from family life and faith to sports, science, history, and literature. She has also written a number of historical and contemporary biographies for young people. She makes her home in Sarasota, Florida.